C0-ARP-729

SERIOUSLY, NOW...

*augsburg publishing house, minneapolis, minn.*

*thought-starters for lent*

# SERIOUSLY, NOW... *by A. Reuben Gornitzka*

seriously, now . . . © augsburg publishing house 1956 . . . manufactured in the united states . . . library of congress catalog card number 56-7247

DEDICATION

This little book
is affectionately dedicated
to my parents
whose inspiration
and example
have constantly
colored my life.

# FOREWORD

On a wall in our house there is a picture that sometimes disturbs me. No, there is nothing wrong with the picture itself. It is only that I find the frame hanging at a tilt on the wall. So on occasion I rather pointedly try to set it right again.

I wonder if you don't find the same sort of thing in your spiritual life. You are suddenly aware that you are off-center spiritually and you need a new point of reference.

The Christian Church down through the years has given to its members a period in the Church year we call "Lent." How wonderfully well it has served in helping us to regain a lost balance. Ever and again we are led back to the core of the Christian Gospel and the saving grace of Jesus Christ. Repeatedly we are jolted out of spiritual lethargy and made to "come alive" in the ever-new freshness of the Spirit.

Perhaps what you find in this little book may be helpful as "thought-starters" for your own devotional life or as "catapults" for talks or sermons. However you may care to use them, let your God-given imagination carry you far out in the circle of God's revealed love.

A limited number of quotations will be found in this book. Sincere attempts have been made to clear these with the writers and publishers in order to give them due credit. Where this has been impossible I beg the gracious understanding of those quoted.

**ACKNOWLEDGMENTS**

The author is indebted to the following for permission to quote from their publications:

Fleming H. Revell Company: Frank C. Laubach's CHANNELS OF SPIRITUAL POWER

Augustana Book Concern: Clifford A. Nelson's sermon in IT WAS FOR YOU

*Collier's:* 1955 Easter editorial and Charles Kettering's "Get Off Route 25, Young Man," December 3, 1954.

# CONTENTS

# A TIME TO REMEMBER

**1**

*a mid-week series for lent*

*And he took bread, and when he had given thanks he broke it and gave it to them, saying, "This is my body which is given for you. Do this in remembrance of Me." And likewise the cup after supper, saying, "This cup which is poured out for you is the new covenant in my blood."* LUKE 22:19-20

Memories can be wonderful things—wonderful in families with birthdays and anniversaries. Memories flood back upon us within a congregation when we observe certain happy events in its history. Memories can be very wonderful, important things.

But memories can also have their heartaches. We discover in the experience of Christian living that memories come which are exceedingly disturbing—memories of certain failures, of temptations that came over us which at the moment we had not the power or will to resist. So back there in the pigeon-holed memory-vault of our minds something is released which needles and annoys.

Now we've discovered that we cannot live peaceably with unresolved memories of sin. It must have been this that brought the Psalmist on one occasion to say, "Lord, remember not the sins of my youth." Even more directly he might have said, "Lord, please forget . . . "

You recall how Paul looked at it when he wrote of "forgetting what lies behind . . . " I am sure that he was thinking at least in part of past sins and failures.

Perhaps you recall the words of a hymn, part of which reads like this:

I look not back, God knows the fruitless efforts,
The wasted hours, the sinning, the regrets,
But I look up, into the face of Jesus,
Who graciously forgives, and then forgets.

(ANNIE JOHNSON FLINT)

That is where you need to look today, if annoying memories are crowding in on you: the unresolved sins which have left scars on your soul, the loss of assurance in your relationship to your heavenly Father.

The only way to forget past sin, sincerely confessed, is to *remember Jesus*. You can forget the past, if you remember Him. And what a One He is for us to remember.

This was the story of one young man. His mother had been a widow in the mountains of Switzerland. He had been her little baby there. Evicted from her home, his mother had taken him in her arms to walk ten miles over the hills to a relative's cottage. She started out in sunshine, but soon a biting snowstorm closed in and she became completely lost.

Strong men forced their way through the next day only to find her nearly naked, her clothes wrapped about a crying bundle as warm with life as she was cold in death.

Years later, a young pastor was preaching an evening sermon in a distant city. This, too, was a cold night with heavy snow and the crowd was small. Reminded of an experience from his father's ministry on an equally miserable night years before, he told the story all over again of the self-sacrificing mother and her baby.

It was a few days later that the pastor found himself at the bedside of a dying man who told him, "I am the son of that widowed mother who died in the snowstorm to protect the life of her little baby. The other night I was stumbling through the streets half-drunk when I slipped in the door and into the back seat of your church. There I heard you tell our story to picture the love of Jesus Christ giving all of Himself for a lost sinner.

"I haven't been able to get that love out of my mind. I've been asking myself what sense it made for my mother to give her wonderful life for me, considering what I turned out to be. And then," he said, "I've been reminded all over again of the love of Jesus Christ who wouldn't let a sinner die. The prayer of my mother has been answered, a prayer that I'm sure she must have prayed, that I would become a child of the Heavenly Father."

That dying man, like us, had two memories, the one of what he was and what he had done; the other of what Jesus Christ is and what He has done.

Friend, never settle alone for the memory of what you are apart from Christ and what you have done in sin to dishonor Him. This is a time to remember what He is and what He has done to make you His child; what He has done with your confessed sin, "Separating it from you as far as the East is from the West, dropping it into the depths of the sea." Remember that "though your sin be as scarlet it shall be white as snow"; that "though it be red like crimson, it shall be as wool."

Perhaps today it will be your privilege to kneel at the communion table. There you will receive the body and blood of your Lord for the remission of your sin. There you will hear your Savior's words, "This do in remembrance of Me."

But to stop here in your remembering can produce a stagnating Christianity which will soon become no Christianity at all. The Christian life is more than just remembering that Christ died for you and made you His child. It is more than just *being;* it is a becoming and a growing. Paul continued this way, "forgetting what lies behind . . . I press on . . ."

Years ago there lived an elderly deacon whose Christian life had stagnated, but who yet sturdily retained the dignity of his Christian standing and experience. "Yes, brethren," he would say, "I'm not making much progress but I'm established." One day in the spring of the year when the frost was coming out of the ground, the deacon set out for town with a heavy load, and became mired. He did his best to get out, but the horses and wagon were thoroughly bogged down in the mud. A neighboring church member coming by stopped to help him. On the basis of the deacon's professed stand, he couldn't resist saying, "Well, deacon, I see that you are not making much progress, but you are established."

Are you remembering *only* the glories of yesterday? Are you remembering only that Christ died for your sins? *Or,* are you remembering with Paul not to be merely established in your spiritual tracks, but to press on . . . on . . . on, "for the prize of the upward call of God in Christ Jesus"?

## A TIME TO LISTEN

**2** *Peter declared to him, "Though they all fall away because of you, I will never fall away." Jesus said to him, "Truly, I say to you, this very night, before the cock crows, you will deny me three times." Peter said to him, "Even if I must die with you, I will not deny you." And so said all the disciples.* MATTHEW 26:33-35

*Then he began to invoke a curse on himself and to swear, "I do not know the man." And immediately the cock crowed.* MATTHEW 26:74

For every Christian there is a time to listen and a time to speak. Peter had a dramatic but heartbreaking experience learning just that.

With his mouth so busy speaking that his ears couldn't hear, Peter failed completely to absorb Jesus' prediction of impending failure. With impetuous over-confidence, Peter declares the sheer impossibility of his denying Christ, however general the desertion by others might be.

But note this: "Likewise also said all the disciples." Peter had company. None was really listening. It was only that he was most vocal. It was almost as though the disciples thought Jesus was merely talking for effect. But the warning was there.

As a child—perhaps even as an adult—was yours ever the experience of being asked to go down to the basement to do something? For a moment when you got there, your mind was a total blank? It was as though you had never been told what you were to do at all?

Peter's experience was something like that. Warming himself by the fire in the courtyard, he is challenged by a mere harmless slip of a girl. Peter denies any relationship to Christ. Challenged again by another maid, he denies even more roughly any connection with this Nazarene. And then again, challenged by several, he curses and swears, and adds, "I tell you I don't know the man." Immediately as the cock crowed, the words of Jesus came back into Peter's mind.

The denial had taken place. The failure was complete. But here again with the crowing of the cock, was a time to listen. This time he did just that. What Jesus had said earlier now suddenly flooded over him. "And he went out and wept bitterly."

As we read these words, you and I wonder, I

suppose, how it was possible that Peter could have failed to hear the warning and then have denied the Christ. But we, too, have often failed to listen to Christ's words of warning or direction. We, too, have then known the experience of being jolted into serious listening when the merciful "cock" has crowed in our hour of defeat.

These are the words of a pencil-scrawled letter from a radio listener, hospitalized as a heart patient and lying, as he said, "with his toes pointed skyward." "Lying this way," he writes, "a person does a lot of thinking. This first experience of mine in a hospital was revealing in that the Lord gave me a recess—but a lot of people had the final bell rung for them. This encounter is the only time I have actually experienced that there comes just a 'God and you' period. Quite an understanding! But in a world of materialism and things coming our way, I guess the average person never gives it serious thought. . . . Of course when business is good and we enjoy health, the vanity of men is such that his ego covers his shoes; so he forgets to be thankful for the ground he walks on and what makes him walk . . . "

Quite a letter! Quite some thinking from a highly successful man in the world of business— but a man for the moment derailed from the ordinary tracks of life, hearing the "cock crow," and *now,* as he added, "listening to an important word from the Lord."

But "the time to listen" is always *now.* Who

knows whether the "cock" of conscience, or illness, or trouble shall crow loudly enough another day? Right today Christ speaks with a word of warning for every casual and self-sufficient Christian, "Pride goes before destruction, and a haughty spirit before a fall." Faith, strength, and power "come by hearing and hearing by the Word of God."

You represent Jesus Christ. As His disciple, you are His representative to the community in which you live. You carry, therefore, a great responsibility. A United States ambassador and friend once said, "You know, one of the things I have discovered is that I have the responsibility of representing the United States of America in such a way as will never bring discredit to my country." What he said was, of course, entirely true. But if true for a nation which we love, how much more true for us as Christians for the Christ we love.

Live close to that Christ. Listen as He warns, inspires, and commands. And should you fail, and the warning "cock" of mercy crow, don't follow Judas to despair, but follow Peter through your tear-dimmed eyes back to your forgiving and revitalizing Savior.

# A TIME TO WAKE UP

**3** *And being in an agony he prayed more earnestly; and his sweat became like great drops of blood falling down upon the ground. And when he rose from prayer, he came to the disciples and found them sleeping for sorrow, and he said to them, "Why do you sleep? Rise and pray that you may not enter into temptation."*

LUKE 22:44-45

Some of the most tragic military defeats in all history have taken place when supposedly there was no enemy around. It was a tremendous military force over which David and his four hundred found victory that night on the desert. The Amalakites celebrating with a drunken brawl their spoiling of David's cities never even dreamed that they had been followed. But the Amalakites were either killed or scattered to the winds.

Where this can happen in the field of the military, it can and does also happen in the world of the spiritual. Any insensitivity to the constant presence of our arch foe, Satan, can place any one of us in an exceedingly dangerous position. We simply cannot afford to take lightly the dead-serious game that the Devil plays, nor can we take lightly the desperate need for a watchful prayer-relationship with Jesus Christ.

It was this that the disciples of Jesus came to learn so dramatically on that night of Christ's betrayal. Unaware of the enemy surrounding them, unaware of the battles ahead of them, these disciples went to sleep. While they slept, Jesus was wrestling in prayer. The end result was that Jesus went on to victory and the disciples, for that time, went on to defeat.

How easy it is for us to be critical of Jesus' followers on that night. But look at us in the world in which we live. Temptations flood in on us from every side, high mountains of them. They come in every modern form, printed, televised, broadcast, whispered, but all of them really only new hats on old sins. It is only much too occasionally that we are very disturbed. How often our casual unawareness is nothing more or less than spiritual sleep.

As the disciples discovered to their heartache, so we too find the Devil to be exceedingly real. One doesn't simply draw a caricature—some horns, a pitchfork, long tail, and hairy body and write him off. He is a real power, determined above all else to conquer the Kingdom of Christ.

The Devil was no joke to Jesus. He had found Satan exceedingly real in that wilderness struggle. Now, as recently as in the Upper Room, Jesus had seen his reality again, for the "supper being ended, the devil now put into the heart of Judas Iscariot to betray Christ."

No wonder then that Jesus was disturbed by the disciples' casual sleepiness. No wonder that he repeated, "Rise and pray, that you may not enter into temptation."

Friends, it is time for us also to wake up. Let me suggest now a few things that we ought to wake up to, and watch out for:

Wake up to the fact that the Devil and his power are real, however much he wants to convince you otherwise. Your Bible won't let you get away from that fact. C. S. Lewis in his book *Screwtape Letters* may help to make this vivid to you.

Wake up to this that the Devil will constantly make a real point of trying to convince you that sin isn't sin. He will blame your failures on environment, heredity, circumstance, everything and anything but sin. What's more, your sinful nature will like and appreciate the explanation.

Wake up to this lie—that what the Devil chooses not to call sin can rather bring you some real happiness and satisfaction. This is one of his greatest lies, which will put you to sleep, only to have you wake up again to the miserable truth that the Devil is a hard task-master.

Just a short time ago newspapers quoted the

words of a stage star who, having attempted the suicide way out for herself and her baby, explained her actions simply in the words, "Life is so hard." The Devil had promised happiness. The Devil is a liar.

Finally, wake up to the Devil's last shot—that, having fallen into sin, there is no way out. Now he can admit that you have sinned, that you have failed your God. He would like to convince you that you are through, that God will have no part of you. He would have you go to sleep now in despair. That is the Devil's story and his final lie.

But here to offset the Devil's lie is God's wondrous truth. In Jesus Christ sin is unmasked for what it is and stripped of what it does. It was nailed to that cross. Its power is finished! Done away!

Through Christ you have been "purchased and won from sin, death and the power of the Devil, in order that you might be His own."

Now, how stay His own? There is one formula so simple that a little child can understand it and do it. Jesus said, "Watch and pray."

In his *Channels of Spiritual Power* Frank Laubach helps us understand these words. He writes, "Wide open upward all the time—and wide open outward all the time. It is allowing ourselves to be wide open channels, ever widening as God stretches us."

When the disciples learned this, they woke up to victory, a victory that has been surging down

14

through the centuries to challenge us. A fine Negro caught it. "Not my father, nor my brother, but it's me, O Lord," he sang, *standing in the need of prayer."*

Standing in the *need* of prayer! Friend, have *you* caught it? Wake up to prayer! Wake up to victory!

15

# A TIME TO CHOOSE

**4** *The governor again said to them, "Which of the two do you want me to release for you?" And they said, "Barabbas." Pilate said to them, "Then what shall I do with Jesus who is called Christ?"*   MATTHEW 27:21, 22

A car is stalled on the railroad tracks. A train is coming. The driver has a choice to make, to stay in or get out. He has the ability to get out if he chooses. Either way there are two possible consequences: Life, if he gets out; death, if he stays in. But all the while that he is making the decision, he is in one of the choices. He is still in the car.

Suppose you are seriously ill. Your illness is diagnosed by the doctor and his verdict is "an operation or death." You have a choice to make, an operation or no operation. You have the ability to choose. The possible consequences are just two, life or death. Yet, all the while you are in the valley of decision, you are moving toward death.

For most of life's decisions, these illustrations are apt pictures. And, with one exception (I will note it later), the same is true of your choosing or rejecting Jesus Christ.

It was a matter of choice that Pilate was wrestling with. How much happier he would have been not to have been faced with it. But he had to choose. No other way to be rid of Christ.

Lest we suggest that this dodging of decision was a monopoly owned by Pilate, we ought to remind ourselves that this sort of thing went on at least four times in the trial of Jesus. It was always someone else's "affair." The high priests had handed Christ over to Pilate. Pilate handed Christ over to Herod. Then it was Herod handing Him back to Pilate.

Now, more nervous than a frightened groom, six times Pilate moves between the courtroom and the crowd at the balcony. If only someone else would make the choice for him. But Herod has been no help. Finally, washing his hands in a theatrical gesture of innocence, Pilate turns Christ over to the mob, pretending that in so doing someone other than he has made the choice. "It is your affair," he says. But for all of time, history records, "crucified under Pontius Pilate."

What a mirror for all mankind is seen in the personality involved in that trial. Jesus Christ is every man's affair, however hard man may seek to evade the issue. Ever and again we want to lay responsibility at another's door-step. We play the game most with our own personal sins and failures. We blame heredity for our sins and say, "I am your affair." We blame environment in the same way with similar excuse. But Christ and what we do with Him is the issue. In this every man has his own responsible choice to make: to receive Christ or reject Him, with the consequence of forgiveness or judgment. And while he delays in his choosing, man is really in one of the choices.

Here are four thoughts for more thinking:

First, every man has a choice to make about Jesus. "The man who is not on my side is against me, and the man who does not gather with me is really scattering" (Phillips), said Jesus. "But why can't I be neutral?" say some. "Because God is a seeking God and is not neutral toward man," is our answer. He has taken the initiative. In Christ "The Expression of God became a human being and lived among us" (Phillips). The heart of Christianity is not man seeking God, but God in Christ seeking man. In essence Christ is asking, "Do you, or do you not want Me?"

So, claim that Christ. By God's grace, believe and confess that Jesus Christ is Lord, and that God raised Him from the dead. "Choose you this day whom you will serve." This calls for positive commitment. It is one thing to acknowledge that Jesus Christ is Lord in a theoretical way. It is quite another to make the choice that you want Him in all the areas of your life. You may be following a kind of religious pattern which leaves you only on the fringe of real commitment without saying, "Lord, take me! I am yours." You are giving Christ no answer for *your* life. And no answer is a "No" answer, bringing you nothing. It takes a "Yes" answer to bring you Life. "The man who is not on my side is against Me, and the man who does not gather with Me is really scattering."

Secondly, to every man to whom the Gospel has come, has also come the *ability* to choose Christ. There are many things in life about which we have nothing to say or even an ability to do. That is true of the color of your eyes, the place you were born, or the length of your nose. But of claiming or denying Jesus Christ, you have both opportunity and ability. When once the Spirit of God through the Gospel has come to you, this is true. Of your own power, neither would you nor could you find and claim Him. But Jesus Christ has chosen you, and in turn given to you the power to respond.

Thirdly, man's choice carries a happy result or a tragic consequence. You can't take just any bus out of town and arrive in New York. By the same token, Jesus is equally logical when He says, "No man comes to the Father *but* by Me."

Does Jesus Christ then condemn those who are by choice outside of Him? We are quickly tempted to say, "Why yes!" But isn't it rather that Christ only judges men on the basis of what they do or do not do with His love?

Does the doctor who accurately diagnoses an illness as fatal unless the patient allows an operation, condemn the patient if the operation is refused? No, the patient really condemns himself. The doctor only presents the saving alternative.

Does Christ condemn the resisting sinner? No, "God sent the Son into the world, not to condemn the world, but that the world might be saved through Him." Christ would love the sinner into heaven. If the sinner does not get there, it is he who has shut himself off from glory. This, then, is the condemnation: that *forgiveness* came in Christ, but a man says "no"; that to a man in darkness, *light* came, but the man pulls the shades of his soul; that to a man lost, the *Way* is come, but man chooses his own footpath.

In our city there used to be a bar with the devilish name of Dante's Inferno, its outer ornamentation suggesting hell itself. It was a reminder of Gypsy Smith's story of a Chicago night club called "Gates of Hell," just doors away from "Calvary Church."

One night a poor drunkard asked a young fellow to show him to the "Gates of Hell." It was pointed out to him with these words of direction: "Just go right by Calvary and you will come to the Gates of Hell."

No one will ever be found in hell simply because he has sinned. Christ came into the world to make that statement possible. Man will be lost to God only because he walks by Calvary! "God so loved the world, that he gave His only Son, that whoever believes in him should not perish but have eternal life.'

# A TIME TO CARRY

**5** *As they were marching out, they came upon a man of Cyrene, Simon by name; this man they compelled to carry his cross.*                    MATTHEW 27:32

*And he who does not take his cross and follow me is not worthy of me.*                    MATTHEW 10:38

A fellow pastor, Clifford A. Nelson, writes of a reproduction in his study of a unique painting done in 1912 by the French artist Jean Beraud, whose attempt was to picture the perpetual nature of the way of the Cross, the Via Dolorosa. Those figures that are crowded about Jesus as He makes His way up that hill so long ago, are not the people of that day but rather of the everyday modern life of 1912. The brutality of these men with their scorn and derision is shown. Others of apparent finer character are there well-dressed and be-

jeweled amidst their gay laughter. Those from
the more rugged ranks of society to those of in-
tellectual dignity are there as well. Even a little
boy picks up a stone to throw.

So very pointedly Beraud dramatizes words I
have long remembered from the pen of Kathryn
Pedley:

> They did not crucify my Lord, one time alone,
> For I have seen Him on that tree,
> Have seen Him bleed and die for me,
> And mocking at his agony, have also thrown a
> stone . . . .

Such an understanding as caught by this artist
and poetess, is one we seek to capture during these
Lenten weeks. Jesus Christ died *because* of me—
because of my sin. He died *for* me—for my salvation.

But there is another great truth in the whole
panorama of the Passion story. I want to confront
you with that. It grows out of the story of Simon
of Cyrene, the man compelled to bear Christ's
cross.

What a shocking experience that must have
been for Simon. How immeasurably humiliated
he must have felt when his shoulder took its
weight. It was in a death-march of "criminals"
that he found himself.

But visualize him later. See the expression on
his face as he hears the strange words, "Father,
forgive them, for they know not what they do."
Watch his facial muscles twitch when the captain

of the guard in astonishment cries, "Truly, this *was* a Son of God." Picture Simon, then as, unlike Pilate, he looks at his cross-dirtied hands wishing that he need never wash them again. Compelled or not, he, Simon, has carried the cross after Jesus.

I wish, as I think of Beraud's thought-provoking painting, that he might have been inspired to paint another. This second, I could wish had been one with Simon of Cyrene carrying the cross in the shadow of Christ. But more than that, to have added the figures of men and women all down the Christian ages, who have also carried the cross after Christ, matching action to His challenge when He said, "If any man would come after me, let him deny himself and take up his cross and follow me." What a thrilling painting that would be.

Picture it. Peter, James, and John would be there—beaten for preaching the Gospel against orders in the market-place. Paul would be there—jailed, persecuted, slandered, finally killed—carrying his cross. Martyrs under Nero's hatred would be there—garden-party torches, arena play-things—carrying their crosses.

Martin Luther would be there—exiled, excommunicated, pressured—carrying his cross.

Modern-day missionaries would be there—persecuted in South America, squeezed out by Communists in China—carrying their crosses.

A negro porter in Grand Central Station would

be there—one who, ridiculed or not, holds daily prayer meetings in an old railroad car; in the face of ridicule—carrying his cross.

A wife and mother of 37 years with a drunken and oft-dangerous husband would be there, loving, praying, sacrificing—carrying her cross.

A Christian couple would be there, living sacrificially to serve Christ better—carrying their cross.

A high school boy would be there, sacrificing certain types of popularity and approval for a Christ-honoring life—carrying his cross.

These and others in an unending list would be there, following in Christ's train, bearing their crosses after Him.

These are they who are building the kingdom of Jesus Christ in our day, our age, and in our back yard. But Jesus Christ who bore that cross to Calvary, and who alone in all the earth can win men back to the heart of God, is looking for a host of others who will join His kingdom cross-bearers.

Jesus Christ makes clear His call for discipleship. We are not with emasculated Christian lives to be comfortable barnacles on the ship of the Church. Nor are we to be soft-souled termites eating away at the structure of the Church, undermining its effectiveness, "indifferent nothings" merely mouthing words, creeds, and hymns. Such Christians in the Church's infancy would never have gotten out of Jerusalem's gates. Such faith certainly would never have arrived in a Twentieth Century America.

A Syrian and an American were aboard a ship in the Mediterranean Sea, chatting and listening to the ship's orchestra. Suddenly, as the sparkling tune, "Parade of the Wooden Soldiers" was heard, the Syrian stood respectfully at attention. Puzzled, the American discovered the friend had thought that melody to be our national anthem.

I do not say this facetiously, but I wonder if there are not times when we of the Church might not look like "wooden soldiers" with that melody a too-apt theme-song. But we are to be soldiers— Christ-men, Cross-men—living heroically and without apology whatever be the price.

Jesus said, "Ye are the salt of the earth," "the light of the world." Salt has "tang" to it. Light has sparkle. Tang and sparkle—these belong to dynamic Christian living. And dynamic Christian living grows out of carrying the cross "after Jesus."

# A TIME TO "SAY SO"

**6** *After this Joseph of Arimathea, who was a disciple of Jesus, but secretly, for fear of the Jews, asked Pilate that he might take away the body of Jesus.*   John 19:38   **29**

*Let the redeemed of the Lord say so.*   PSALM 107:2

A passenger aboard a commuter train found himself very curious. An elderly gentleman moving slowly down the aisle was leaning over and quietly whispering something to each passenger. When the old gentleman came to him, these were the words he heard: "Excuse me, but if anyone in your family is blind, tell him to see Dr. Back. He gave me back my sight."

There is something very wonderful about telling someone else about great things or great people that happen into our lives. But it makes you wonder in reading the Passion history how it could be that not a single voice was lifted then in Christ's defense. All one hears are the re-echoing words, "Crucify Him, crucify Him."

Never would there have been a better time to hear again, "Hosanna to the Son of David, blessed is he that cometh in the name of the Lord." Where was the Palm Sunday crowd?

Or, where the voices of the ten lepers whose lives had been totally changed? Where the widow of Nain?—the blind man of Jericho? Where the disciples? Where Lazarus? Where those miraculously fed on the mountain, those who had been demon possessed? Where was the bubbling story of their hearts? Here was a time for these and countless others to "say so," but they didn't.

Now I'm not one bit sure that you or I would have done any better had we been there. But I want to think a bit with you of what it can mean for Christ and His Church, if we who know the Lord in much easier days are "crazy thankful," and then by witness of word and life "say so."

Paul expressed it very crisply once. He said, "For I am not ashamed of the Gospel: it is the power of God for salvation to every one who has faith." At the time of Jesus' trial, His followers weren't that convinced. Joseph of Arimathea wasn't. He was a disciple, "but secretly, for fear," as are many today. Now Joseph didn't remain that. Quite remarkable when you realize that with Christ's death, Joseph steps into "the open" to make what must have appeared a really thorough-going fool of himself.

Well, "a fool for Christ's sake" is just what Joseph and Paul became. They were God's kind of fools. And that is a pretty good kind to be.

A man carrying what is called a "sandwich board" (a sign hanging in front of him and another to the rear, usually for advertising) was seen walking a city street. In front the board read, "A fool for Christ's sake." On the rear, for the benefit of ridiculing strollers, were the words, "Whose fool are you?" And the truth is that we are all somebody's fool, either in a miserable way, Satan's or in an exciting way, Christ's.

Now Paul was saying in essence that, first, he was not ashamed of Jesus Christ. It's easy for us to ask, "Why should he be?" We say that there was no other figure in all history like Him. We add that no one has ever been able to point an accusing finger in His direction; that none has healed the sick, raised the dead, comforted the sorrowing, and beyond all else crushed the head of sin and death as He did. But have *you* never been ashamed or apologetic about Jesus?

Nor was Paul ashamed of Christ's Gospel. Again we find it easy to ask, "Why should he?" Again we say that there is no other message in all history like His. Who else has gone into the darkest corners of the world and turned the light on? Who else has transformed human personalities so that they are scarcely recognizable over against their old selves? Who else has given such strength to the sick, such hope to the dying? Who else has lifted men above the puny goals of success, power, bank accounts, and pleasure? Who else saves men's souls? But have *you* never been ashamed of that same Gospel?

Wonderful, when we can say with Paul, "I am not ashamed of the Gospel," because we know it as being "the power of God for salvation" in our life. When that is true, then what happened in the contagious enthusiasm of the early Christians begins to happen in our lives. We declare our crowning allegiance to Jesus Christ, and enthusiastically "say so." Christian loyalty and enthusiasm are wonderful things.

What kind of enthusiasm comes with the keys when you get a new car? Class, power, pick-up, comfort—you have a whole story to tell enthusiastically.

Or listen to the radio, the portable loud-speakers, watch the "ads" and billboards when elections roll around. There is enthusiasm there.

You should have heard the cheers and school songs as they exploded at a football banquet I attended recently. No apologies there, just unadulterated enthusiasm and loyalty.

Now what of the enthusiasm of our Christian life? Sometimes when I look at it I am reminded of the story of an older couple in Norway. The sailor husband, returning from a year's absence, greeted his wife at the door by shaking hands.

Quite a contrast to the couple a certain father overheard on the front porch: "For two cents I'd kiss you," said the young man. "Well, here's fifty cents," replied the girl. There was enthusiasm even though a bit left of center.

But we in the Church of Jesus Christ can afford to show a great deal more genuine, unashamed, down-to-earth enthusiasm for our Lord than most of us have begun to reveal.

All around us there are spiritually crippled men and women who need help from radiant Christians to get them into the pool of Christ's Church. And the best argument visible to the world for Christianity is still the Christian whose life is a "living letter, known and read of all men."

The time for you and for me to "say so" for Christ is *now*. Our Lord is still being "crucified afresh" to right and to left of us. If the voices of the redeemed aren't heard, the voices of the enemy will prevail. Disciples, "secretly, for fear," don't count. *Now* is the time to "say so."

# THE HOUR HAS COME

## 7

*When Jesus had spoken these words, he lifted up his eyes to heaven and said, "Father, the hour has come; glorify thy Son that the Son may glorify thee."* JOHN 17:1     35

Three years can be a long time if you are waiting for something important. If you were two years old and your sister, five, was in kindergarten, three years would be a long wait. Or, three years is a long time for the college sophomore who is eagerly awaiting the hour when preparation days are over, and when life seemingly can begin in earnest. Three years is a long time for the girl in love who has to wait until her future husband comes back from service.

It probably had seemed a long time for the disciples of Jesus, though probably too so very short as they looked back on it in later years. But they had, as it were, been "holding their breaths" throughout all of the three-year ministry of Jesus. What was coming? What lay in their future? They weren't quite sure.

For good or bad, something was going to happen. Anxiously, tensely, they waited as time and again Jesus cooled their mistaken ardor for an earthly king, or relaxed their fear-tensed hearts with, "My hour has not yet come. . . . . "

The days rolled up into weeks, weeks into months, months into these three years. One day the story changed. Jesus had brought Lazarus out of the grave. All about Him there was excitement; disciples and countless others were thrilled by what had taken place. But not all thrilled. Not all were in happy wonder. For behind the doors of temple chambers, the Pharisees futilely having tried to discredit the Christ were now saying, "Perceive ye how ye prevail nothing. Behold the whole world is going after Him." Then it was that Jesus said at long last, "The hour is come that the Son of Man should be glorified."

This was it. *Now* something was going to happen. No more wondering. No more waiting. No more slipping away. No more living in the hills and dodging Jerusalem as they had much of the time. Jesus wasn't taking this enmity, this sneering, this defiance any more. Israel wasn't going to have to take this rotten Rome any more with slavery, disgrace—they, Israel, the chosen people of God. And who would stop this Jesus? Hadn't

He made water into wine? Hadn't He fed thousands on a mountainside with a fistful of food? Hadn't He raised Lazarus from the dead? Hadn't He walked on water? What could stop Him? This was it. *The hour had come,* or so they thought.

But it wasn't *their* kind of hour, was it, nor yours nor mine? It wasn't their kind of "glorifying" either. For those words—about a grain of wheat falling into the ground and dying in order to bring forth fruit—weren't just conversation. They were about Jesus Christ. *He* was going to die. *He* was going to be buried. And what kind of glory is that? The hour has come. But what kind of an hour?

You and I know this answer, we who stand on this side of that 1900-year-old cross. We know. We ought to know. The disciples of Jesus, in their eager and quite blinded anticipation, had forgotten what Jesus had said. He had said, "And as Moses lifted up the serpent in the wilderness, even so must the Son of man be lifted up, that whosoever believeth on him should not perish but have eternal life"—that God gave His only begotten Son, . . . . . and "not to condemn the world, but that the world through him might be saved."

But there were other words too. "Let not your heart be troubled, ye believe in God, believe also in me. In my Father's house are many mansions, I go to prepare a place for you. And if I go and prepare a place for you, I will come again and receive you unto myself, that where I am there ye may be also." Glorified? "Glorify Thy Son that Thy Son may glorify Thee."

Well, maybe there was a greater glory than what they had been thinking about. Maybe there was a whole lot more to "glory" than being earthly king over a puny nation ruled by arrogant Romans. What about eternal life? What of forgiveness for a whole world of men, for people of every age? That sounded like a real glory, whatever way the road would take to arrive there.

This was the way. Before Christ lay an ugly cruel cross, a cross made of sin and all the independent rebelliousness of the souls of men for all time. That's what lay in that hour—God in His Son, Satan in man, met in mortal conflict. Into that struggle of the eternities stepped the Christ. God's time-clock on sin had run out. Man needed saving. Here, in Christ, was the Savior.

Now the cross is fact. It's history. But it's not a cold, dead fact. It's not just past history. It's also a very real fact for your day, for mine. The cross today stares you in the face. Look at it; you cannot stare it down. It says, "You are a sinner. I wouldn't be, were it not for you, for sin. Your sin helped hang the Christ here. Your sin helped drive the nails through His hands, His feet. You helped drop this cross with a sickening jolt into the hole dug in the ground here at Calvary. You made me, ugly as I am." So says the cross.

But with all the fury of hell here, with all the

agony, the pain, the mockery and ridicule, the hour of this can mean glory for you. Christ didn't have to die here. He chose this hour. He said, "Father, Thy will be done." He *said* it— He *did* it —He *did* it, for *you.*

The hour has come for man too, the hour when rebelliously indifferent man can't play with the clock any more. It is the hour for man to kneel before that cross. Individually we must decide whether we will glorify the Christ, accepting Him, living in His forgiving grace, or reject Him and miss the glory of life.

We stand at a cross-roads, whether individual men or nations. Those words may sound old and meaningless, but they remain true. The world is facing judgment, if not God's, man's own judgment upon himself. We've said that we would somehow "muddle through" when we faced a crisis. But we won't. We won't muddle through a saving of our own selves. No, the answer lies only in the cross of Christ, His forgiveness, His life, His hope, His power. And in that cross of Christ alone will we find real glory, or we shall find none at all.

Nor shall the world we want to live in. Christ prayed, "Father, glorify thy Son that thy Son may also glorify thee." Something like that must be our prayer too. "Father, lead us to glory through salvation in Christ. Lead us to power. Lead us to usefulness. Lead us to compassion for lost souls. Lead us to righteousness, that we might also glorify Thee." We need Christ. We cannot live without Him.

The hour has come. It's the hour of the cross. It's here. The time is *now*.

During one of the past days, a husband and wife came to my study to say something. It went something like this. "We have believed in God. We belong to the church. We confess that we have been poor church members. We have lived independently of God and thought we could solve our own problems, and satisfy our own needs. We have both of us together discovered all too well that we can't. Now we want to begin all over, together. We want to find the meaning of real, assured forgiveness. We want to live our lives with real purpose. We want to be positively, actively, meaningfully Christian. Won't you help us?"

For that couple, life's greatest hour had come.

# OUT OF A SPIRITUAL RUT

8

*I can do all things in him who strengthens me.*
PHILIPPIANS 4:13



You and I live in a world in which so-called physical impossibilities are constantly becoming possibilities. The last generation or two has known some real surprises: sulphas, penicillins, jet planes, television, and atom bombs.

Few of us in our day dare to talk about physical impossibilities in a world of medical, mechanical, and general scientific genius. Not even when they talk of future trips to the moon do we dare chuckle very loudly. Even what we cannot explain, we now accept as quite possible.

I'm afraid, however, that altogether too many of us are not nearly so far along in our vision and beliefs in the spiritual world. We don't strive for very much spiritual knowledge. We don't often aspire to very much true holiness. We don't dream very great dreams of courage, faith, and vision. "It can't be done," we say. Although our God has flatly stated and distinctly proven that certain glorious things can be real for our Christian experience, we doubt, question, or minimize. We continue to live on in the unexciting drabness of half-claimed promises; in the uninteresting ruts of a visionless faith which dares not test the Lord.

It is to such as we that Paul's seemingly impossible claim in Philippians 4:13 comes as a jolt. He writes from a prison-house in Rome, "I can do all things through Christ which strengtheneth me." "I can do all things," he suggests. There are great possibilities for us, he says, "through Christ."

Perhaps our difficulty, boiled down to pea size, amounts to this, that we haven't really caught those crucial words, "through Christ."

Charles Kettering (Boss Kett, as he is affectionately known to his friends), the automotive genius of General Motors, tells of this incident in a *Colliers* article. An engineer friend at the General Motors Detroit plant had a home near Dayton, Ohio, where his family lived, even as did Mr. Kettering. One day as they visited together at the plant, Kettering stated that it took him four and one-half hours to drive each way when he went home week-ends. The friend flatly questioned either his memory or his honesty, saying that it couldn't be done. Kettering's response was to invite the friend to drive with him the next weekend. They made the trip together. They did make it in four and one-half hours. The engineer friend registered little amazement at the driving time, however, because, as he said, "You didn't drive Route 25. You took another route."

Kettering's reply was to the effect that there had been no discussion as to what route. All they had talked about was driving time. The fact that he was wise enough to substitute another highway for the heavily travelled Route 25, had been no part of the discussion. To the engineer friend, Kettering's four and one-half hours was impossible until he discovered that their way of accomplishing an identical thing was altogether different. The impossible became possible.

Kettering's moral, as he points it out after telling the story was, that we ought to get off some of the commonplace, visionless, courageless "Route 25s" and discover how the impossibles can be made the possibles.

I think that this fits the realm of the spiritual very well. Our spiritual sights are low. Our spiritual experiences are limited. An expansion to a truly Christlike life is often hampered. We are stuck with the old human, earthly, worldly Route 25 of self-achievement, of believing that if a thing doesn't make sense humanly speaking, we can't reach it; if we can't achieve it by sheer will power, by our strivings, then it just isn't possible. We ought neither to concern ourselves nor bother our minds very much about it.

Let me point out in some concrete ways what I mean. I say that *it is possible* through Christ for those who are willing to grasp the very real power of the Lord to lead a life in which His promises, taken as they stand, are found to be true.

First of all, it is possible for mortal men and women, through Christ, and in spite of being sinners, to arrive at a clear-cut assurance of a right relationship to God. How tragically many there are who, when speaking of their future destiny, speak only in terms of a vague sort of hope. It is as though they were stuck with some earthly Route 25 philosophy of *aspiring* to find God, but have never consciously accepted in faith the clear-cut route *through Christ.* Through Christ a human impossibility becomes a gloriously promised divine possibility.

The Devil, and the natural human heart, say, "Impossible! There must be something I must do." God's Word says, "There is therefore now no condemnation to them that are *in* Christ Jesus." "When our hearts condemn us God is greater than our hearts." "If we confess our sins, he is faithful and just to forgive us our sins and to cleanse us from all unrighteousness." As a result of such saving grace, there surely ought to follow a deep desire to live a holy life.

Secondly, it is a divine possibility to be made

holy, to have thoughts of hearts purified. Here, following our experience of the saving grace of Christ, too many of us again bog down in the ruts of the humanly impossibles. Here our problem strikes us this way. (The Devil is the author of such thinking, of course.) "Be ye holy, for I am holy," we read. "Oh," but I say, "I can't be. It just isn't in me to be. I've tried. I've failed again and again. I give up. I'll just have to do the best I can."

But where have we found ourselves now? We are back on Route 25. This is the route where after a time of feeble attempt and failing resolution, we conclude that it doesn't make too much difference. We will just hope for the best. Holy living belongs to some other rather rare and somehow (but we don't know how) saintly personalities.

But hear me now! God's unchanged and unchanging inspired and inspiring Word says, "My God shall supply all your need, according to his riches in glory by Christ Jesus." Again, "I commend you to God and to the Word of his grace which is able to build you up, and to give you an inheritance among all them that are sanctified."

Whatever, then, your sin may be, hold still in the presence of the living God. There *is* victory through Christ—victory over pride, victory over selfishness, over impure desires, over thoughtlessness, unkindness, a gossipy slanderous tongue. All these sins the devil tells us we can never defeat are sins every one of which the Lord will defeat when you claim His promises. It *is* possible.

Among the divine possibilities promised by the Almighty God to His children is that you can leave all your cares with Him and enjoy a deep peace in doing so.

I wonder if there is a single soul who has in Christian faith honestly lived with faith in such promises and found them to be untrue. Certainly there have been scores of folks in moments of extreme desperation who have called upon a God (who was little more than a stranger, and before whom they have never bowed a repentant knee) who would list God's care among the world's impossibilities. But I wonder if there have been any who, coming in sincere and humble faith, have not found that the promises of God stand sure, that His loving care is very real. "My God shall supply all your need." Do we believe this to be a divine possibility? It is.

Are these things possible? Of course they are, *possible* through Christ whose "grace is sufficient for all our needs"; through Christ who enabled His servant of old, and servants since, to say, "I *can* do all things through Christ which strengtheneth me."

# LIFT UP YOUR EYES

**9** *Come to me, all who labor and are heavy-laden, and I will give you rest.* MATTHEW 11:28

High over the entrance to our church is seen the 16-foot stone figure of "The Inviting Christ." It is a strong figure, yet warm and appealing. With hands outstretched, though with unspoken words, the invitation moves out over the busy avenue, "Come Unto Me." Each day the occupants of 35,000 cars passing by are reminded of this greatest invitation ever extended to man. Sun-lighted by day and flood-lighted by night, the invitation is always there.

For nineteen centuries now Jesus Christ has held out this invitation to the world. It has come to the Mediterranean area with its cloudless skies but oft-shadowed hearts. It has come to lands of blinding snows with souls cooped up in spiritual igloos and twenty-four-hour nights. It has come to the jogging rickshaw driver in the Orient, to the executive at a Wall Street desk; to the deckhand in a New Zealand port. Wherever He has gone, He has said, "Come Unto Me."

I'm glad that Jesus Christ has invited me to come to Him. I'm glad first of all *because if He hadn't I should have been afraid to come.* Someone might ask, "But how could that be possible? Wasn't it this Christ who came into the world for sinners?" And I would say, "That's true, of course." Then I would be asked, "Didn't Christ when He hung on that cross, wrap, as it were, His arms about the whole sinful world in tender love and forgiveness?" And I would say again, "Yes, that's true, of course." And then I would add, "But you see I sometimes feel like the Prodigal Son who said, 'I am not worthy to be called thy son; make me a servant . . . .' Or I feel like Peter when, overwhelmed by the holiness of Christ, he fell at Jesus' feet and said, 'Depart from me for I am a sinful man, O Lord.' Sometimes I'm afraid to come. It seems so ridiculous that Christ would bother any longer with me."

But there *is* something Jesus said that does take me over even such blocks as these in my heart. That something is found in His words, "and him who comes to me I will not cast out." "Whoever" comes. That does it. That reaches out to me too. I am not now afraid to come.

Secondly, I am glad that Jesus keeps inviting me, *because I don't always feel like coming,* and I need to. His invitation reminds me that He always has something for me.

It is peculiar how many of us there are who on occasion think that Christ is going to rob us of something we like, rather than give us something we need. As such we stay away for fear of becoming involved. How foolish we can be! For taking His yoke and learning of Him is always an expansive experience of moving out into a fuller life. It is never a cramped prison. "His yoke is easy, and His burden is light" is totally in contrast to my imprisoned self-life.

Thirdly, I am glad for the words, "Come Unto Me," *because when spiritually tired, I need a place to rest.* All I have to do is struggle in a legalistic "rightness" of my own to get all worn out. There, more than anywhere else, I need rest. Just as heavy a burden can crush my shoulders here as the burden of the man enslaved by gross sin and with no God-consciousness at all: the burden of goodness for goodness' sake, the burden of loving with a loveless heart, the burden of service with a stilted soul.

On the cross He said, "It is finished!" There is nothing I can add to His saving work or my "righteousness." I can respond, however, with Christian growth and spiritual service when my life is impowered by His life within me. It is at this point I find rest. In Christ lies peace for my heart.

Now, lest we become confused in our "peace of soul" age, let's remember that while "rest" is something very real when in Christ I am reconciled to God, there is another sense in which this "rest" may lead me on to a healthy "restlessness," a certain inner turbulence. Spiritual "rest" in Christ does not allow me to atrophy on a spiritual *chaise-longue*. My experience of "rest" in Christ leads me to a discontent over my own spiritual sluggishness and to a concern for the individual, the community, and the world about me. I am not in a vacuum free from spiritual laziness, temptation, and trouble, nor from opportunity and responsibility. But in Christ I find the grace to meet them.

Finally, I'm glad for Christ's invitation, because every time I have humbly accepted it and receptively come, *I've found what Christ promised.* Jesus said, "If any man thirst, let him come unto me and drink. . . . . " "He who believes in me, out of his heart shall flow rivers of living water." "I came that they may have life, and have it abundantly."

These are not mere words. All of the treasures of heaven are Christ's to share with His own. All of His powers are reservoirs to draw on. Doubting His promises, we have often gone empty away. Believing and claiming them, we have moved into the new world of the abundant life.

# WONDERFULLY DIFFERENT

**10**

*I have given them thy word; and the world has hated them because they are not of the world, even as I am not of the world. I do not pray that thou shouldst take them out of the world, but that thou shouldst keep them from the evil one.*          JOHN 17:14-15

Have you become "wonderfully different" because of the cross? That is just what happened to Peter.

I have in my possession a painting which is a visual sermon all in itself. It is a gift from an artist member of the congregation, whose original work it is. When I first saw it, there was no need for the artist to tell me either who or what was represented. It was of Peter at the moment when the cock crowed and he looked up into the face of Jesus.

Deep sadness was etched on this large, rugged, and weatherbeaten face. Tears had welled up in his eyes. Disappointing defeat and heartache were the theme.

I couldn't forget that face once I had seen it. The next day I sat down with my Bible and read the two letters of Peter written long after that courtyard hour. I was particularly struck by the first, addressed to believers living in a day of persecution under Nero. Hearts of men were being tried. Faith needed to be strengthened.

Would these Christians suffer martyrdom, rather than deny their Lord? This was a vital question for the early Church, and a real concern in Peter's mind. So it was that Peter, once over-bold yet weak, impetuous yet fearful, now writes encouragingly out of new experiences of victory.

He speaks of being guarded by the power of God operating through his faith for a salvation; of the tremendous joy of being born again into a life full of hope even though at present he and his fellow-Christians were "temporarily harassed by all kinds of trials and temptations." Peter says, "They happen to prove your faith, which is infinitely more valuable than gold, and gold as you know, even though it is ultimately perishable, must be purified by fire. This proving of your faith is planned to bring you praise and honor and glory in the day when Jesus Christ reveals Himself " (Phillips).

Can you imagine the Peter of the courtyard

and of that heartache and defeat as being this same Peter who now can write of temptations as proving his faith to praise and honor and glory?

As I read these words, I wish I might have a second painting, a companion picture of this man who had become so "wonderfully different" through the miracle of God's grace and power.

A little girl in India, asked about the Christians that she knew, described them as "the folks who are different." "Wonderfully different!" That description ought to hold good in any land and in any age.

Why? Two reasons: first, because Jesus Christ, source of Christian life, is "wonderfully different" from any other. He is the Son of God. Secondly, because in Christ man becomes a "new creation." "Old things are passed away." The Christian becomes a part of a "new world."

During the closing years of his life, Wendell Willkie was known not least for the phrase, "One World." Yes, that in one sense is the kind of global atmosphere we live in today, joined together by miracles of science to mere hours apart by plane, only minutes and seconds by telegraph, telephone, and television. Yet, there are other things which separate nations and peoples so that in reality we are not "one world" as we would like to believe.

This is true in the realm of the spiritual as well. There are in fact "two worlds" in which we humans live. Jesus suggests this so clearly in His

53

great prayer. Part of it is found in St. John, Chapter 17. "I have given them thy word; and the world has hated them because they are not of the world, even as I am not of the world."

This is not mere theological philosophizing. Jesus spoke so clearly of it. "Ye *are* of this world," He said to the Pharisaical critics. Of His own He said, "They are *not* of this world." There is then a world of the Spirit in which those who know, love, walk, and talk with God live.

For some this might suggest that Christians live in a sort of vacuum, cooped up in sheltered cloisters, withdrawn from the realities—hothouse plants, if you will. But this fits neither what Jesus did nor what He said. Out of the glory and wonder of heaven He came into all the reality of this world. He said, "I do not pray that thou shouldst take them out of the world, but that thou shouldst keep them from the evil one." We live *in* one world but *belong* to another, a higher world. As such, and because this is true, we are to be, and can be, "wonderfully different."

Someone, somewhere, has told of a tiny animal that lives in mud puddles, but really belongs in the air. It is able to live in the mud because it makes an air-bladder which it drags along the bottom and breathes that air while surrounded by muddy water.

What a helpful picture of the Christian's life in the Spirit while in the world. Surrounded by "air" from above, which is the Holy Spirit, he is still able to "breathe," and more than breathe, to live with power though impurity crowds around him. But how does such an amazing thing take place? The answer lies in the Word. Here alone can be found the message of forgiveness. What can be more effective for the repentant soul than the promise "If we confess our sins, he is faithful and just to forgive us our sins and to cleanse us from all unrighteousness." My assurance of forgiveness then does not lie in wishful thinking, but in that of which the Holy Spirit is able to convince me through the Word.

And power lies here in this Word. Faith is not something that I can manufacture. "Faith cometh by hearing, and hearing by the Word of God." Again the Holy Spirit through the Word brings about a basically important result in my spiritual experience. In the Word, "I live and move and have my being" as a Christian. Without the "air" from above, the Holy Spirit working through the Word, I cease to "breathe." Surrounded by it, fed and vitalized by it, I live.

This is it, "Wonderfully Different." Not a miracle of human ingenuity, but a miracle of God's amazing grace.

# THE CROSS AGAINST THE SKY

**1** *For the word of the cross is folly to those who are perishing but to us who are being saved it is the power of God.* I CORINTHIANS 1:18

I was driving east on a highway in southern Tennessee and climbing the slopes of the beautiful Cumberland mountains. Suddenly I noticed in the distance high above me at the center of a large clearing in the forest a huge white cross. Just as those who had erected it had intended, I began to think.

How very differently those viewing that cross would react. One driver seeing it, would discover an unconscious response of love. All that the cross of Christ meant would flood over him. With the hymn writer, words would form on his lips, " . . . for I love that old cross, where the dearest and best for the world of lost sinners was slain." His heart would respond with grateful love.

Another driver, he too one of Christ's, might react with a moment of intense shame. Perhaps an experience of that day, or of a night before, some shoddy business deal, some careless act might suddenly loom large. A new sensitivity to sin might move into his soul. "Crucifying the Son of God afresh," are no longer mere words, but a new experience. The man's spirit might carry him kneeling to the Christ. Blurted out are words which plead, "God be merciful to me, a sinner."

Another driver looks through his windshield at the scene on the mountain. For long days hope has been gone from his soul. That cross had had meaning to him when he was a child. As an adult he has failed totally to relate Christ and His cross to himself and his sins. Christianity, to him, has been for the mentally sick, the emotionally starved hangers-on, the weak parasites of society.

And what of himself? With increasing rapidity, life has been turning to ashes in his hands. His own adequacy has become no adequacy at all. Sin and guilt are scratched all over the pages of his life. Failure has become his theme-song. His very self has been disintegrating. Hope is all but gone.

But there before his eyes is the cross. Forgiveness is to be found there. He remembers that now. And more than just forgiveness, power is to be had there—"the cross . . . . the *power* of God." Too late? Maybe not. For hadn't he in Sunday school once memorized some words that read, "Whosoever cometh unto me, I will in no wise cast out"? And a song begins to fill the ear, remembered words from mother's knee—"Just as I am without one plea . . . wilt welcome, pardon, cleanse, relieve . . . O Lamb of God, I come . . . . "

A fourth driver moves along the same highway. He, too, sees the cross on the mountainside. But his are really unseeing eyes. Were the casual, unspoken remark of inner-being to have been heard, the words would only have been, "Some foolishness, that." Nor would he have been the first or last to react that way

"Some foolishness" was also the response of many to the cross in Paul's day. No sense of sin and guilt before a holy God means no sense of need for the saving Christ. Only the drowning have a critical interest in life-preservers. Only the consciously lost seek desperately to be found.

Are you spiritually drowning? Are you lost and need to be found? John reminds us, "If we say that we have no sin, we deceive ourselves and the truth is not in us. If we confess our sins, he is faithful and just and will forgive our sins and cleanse us from all unrighteousness."

One cross-hung robber didn't know he was lost. He therefore had no concern for being found. The other sensed his need and claimed his answer —Jesus Christ. To the one, the cross and Christ were "some foolishness." To the other, the cross brought the power of God.

## LET CHRIST BE KING, NOW

## 12

*Tell the daughter of Zion, Behold, your king is coming to you, humble, and mounted on an ass, and on a colt, the foal of an ass. . . . And the crowds that went before him and that followed him shouted, "Hosanna to the Son of David! Blessed be he who comes in the name of the Lord! Hosanna in the highest!"*     MATTHEW 21:5, 9

Whether you or I or anyone else likes it or not, Jesus Christ *is* King—"King o'er all the earth." It is only a question of whether He is also King of your heart, *now*.

How angry the religious leaders in Jerusalem must have been when their newshawks burst through the doors on that first Palm Sunday. "The people have gone crazy. They've started a parade for that trouble-maker Jesus. They've made a carpet of their robes and palm branches and are shouting 'Hosanna, blessed is the king of Israel, that cometh in the name of the Lord.'"

"Jesus—King? Never!" might well have been the reply from the muttering enemies within the temple walls. "We will fix him, frame him, get rid of him before the week is out. Then we will see what kind of a king he is—dead!"

No one on earth would be more startled than these same men, were it possible for them to attend church today. Imagine the expressions on their faces were they to merely stand at the doors of our churches and watch millions of this King's subjects file past. Picture them stepping inside to hear the Palm Sunday Gospel being read in more than a thousand languages and dialects all over the world—in a straw-roofed chapel in Africa, in an ice-coated igloo in northern Alaska, on the sunny deck of an aircraft carrier in the Pacific. Put them within the hearing of a Christian broadcast, within sight of a televised service; they who were so sure He would not be King. Dead before the week was out? Yes, but with Easter morning He rose again to ride on in love, conquering human hearts, King for all eternity.

Man, you see, really has no vote as to whether Christ will be king, not in this election. However you may or may not relate Christ to your own life, you cannot exile Him like a Duke of Windsor to some distant shore and write Him off. He is still around. And on that great day in eternity it will be before that Kingly Christ that we shall have to answer for our own stupid attempts to be our own little kings.

How impressed men have been with their supposed ability to write Christ in or out of life. Picture the humble setting that morning when Jesus was having late "coffee" with Martha, Mary, and Lazarus in little Bethany. Not much to impress you. No high-ranking cabinet members in conference. No pompous officers standing at attention before glittering ranks. Just Jesus and His friends, some soon on their way to borrow a donkey for the Jerusalem ride.

By contrast, high priests had their servants bowing and scraping in the temple court. Pilate's battalions marched in lock-step through the streets. Cavalry-men on great white horses kicked dust in the peasants' faces. Herod pulled his purple robe close about him as he sat at breakfast on the palace patio. Caesar seated himself on his gold throne in the marble palace at Rome, temporarily ruler of the world. But the "King o'er all the earth" was in a cottage, ready soon to ride the city streets and offer His reign of love one last time.

How temporary a reception! How futile seemed His acclaim that day in the light of the happenings that week. But only if you stop with Good Friday, for the measuring stick of the success of Christ's reign as King is not to be found in that week. It is to be found at the empty tomb on Easter morn

—or far better on Palm Sunday of 1956, and most completely "when Jesus comes in glory as Lord and King of kings."

Temporariness and futility is not to be found in Christ the King, but in men who choose to be their own little kings. How often the devil must chortle over such little kings: mere puppets dangling from his strings, but all the while believing themselves to be the puppeteer.

Let's not think that the Devil hasn't had his hours of laughter as he has watched men struggle to educate themselves out of their problems, only to vote more penitentiaries, more detention homes, more divorce courts. As he has watched men seek to bury their troubles under an avalanche of frenzied pleasures, with more sex, more liquor, more thrills, and more things. As he has watched men struggle to power their way out of their fears with "A" bombs, "H" bombs, cobalt bombs, international ballistic missiles.

But have these made men more secure? Have pleasures satisfied starving souls? Has wisdom taught men how to live with God or one another, internationally or in our own back-yards? Has physical power set men free?

These are the words of a *Collier's* editorial, April 15, 1955. ". . . . the scientist, once serenely confident he had mastered the secrets of the universe, unlocked the atom and discovered an astonishing new universe. . . . Unlocking such doors can be humbling; out of such humility springs reverence.

"The statesman, seeking the means of bringing order to the world's affairs, has been abruptly confronted with forces too vast to respond to the time-worn processes of nations and diplomats. Contemplating these surging movements of history, he senses the need for a key, an answer beyond his own wisdom.

"The ordinary man, used to bringing ordinary solutions to ordinary problems, finds his once placid world brought to the very eve of doomsday, by forces quite beyond his capacity to grasp or his power to control. He too senses keenly the imperativeness of a sure source of guidance."

The article then adds, "What they all seek—the hand of God—has been available through all the centuries. It is there now to grasp. . . . . "

Startling? Of course such comments are. When else in history have such things as these and others been written in such dimensions, attracting as wide readership, as in our day? Atom-bomb scare? Perhaps, but more than that, a realization that puny, finite minds, seeking after solutions to mountainous problems and sins piled upon the souls of men and nations, will find no answer until Christ is King in human hearts.

You *can't* ignore God's natural rule in the handiwork of His creation. You *can't* plant water-melon seeds and have them come up radishes. You can't change God's moral rule, for wrong will not indefinitely come out right. Yet you *can* in this life escape the rule of Jesus Christ in your heart if you choose. But in doing so, you keep yourself outside the "city-limits" of the city of God. It is your choice to make. He has chosen you, has tried to woo and win your allegiance. But He forces no will of His upon you. He has given you both power to claim Him and the right to deny Him your allegiance. But whatever the world or you or I do about His kingship for our lives, He will still be on *His* throne, if not on the throne of our hearts.

Palm Sunday is a day for happy subjects of the King to thrill to. It is a day for proclaiming Christ, not alone as Savior who has redeemed me, but as Lord and Master who rules my subject-heart.

Friend, whatever may come to this old world of ours, nothing is so important as this, your allegiance to Jesus Christ, your awareness of His kingly power, your living in the constant assurance of His eternal reign. You are no serf, no spiritual peasant under despotic rule. You are a son and heir of the King. So straighten your back. Lift your head high. Walk with a sure step. You belong to the eternal, undefeatable, loving and ever-powerful King of kings.

# YOUR BRIDGE, NOW

## 13

*Jesus said to him, "I am the way, and the truth, and the life; no one comes to the Father, but by me."* JOHN 14:6

God built a bridge, the most awesome ever built, with the longest span across the widest chasm in the world.

Now material bridges have belonged to almost all of time. In man's earliest days, I suppose, he found that nature had created the first bridge for him, a clinging vine by which he swung his way from one side of a river or gorge to another. Then he found himself a fallen log dropped across a stream. Balancing his way he found himself on what you might call a bridge.

Time moved on. Man was seen piling stone upon stone to form a new kind of bridge. From here man moved from level to arch bridges, from eighteenth century cast-iron structures to nineteenth century steel bridges, and finally to the great suspension bridge with its huge cables hung from tower to tower.

We have crossed on some of these, you and I, perhaps unconsciously open-mouthed in awe and wonder. These are marvels from the hand of man.

But I am thinking of one bridge today which is a bridge more important than all others, spanning an even wider chasm, a deeper gorge, swifter rapids—and it is the bridge which God Himself laid down in giving Jesus Christ to a mankind separated hopelessly from Him by sin.

The separation began with the fall of man in the Garden of Eden. Where man had stood by the side of the Holy God, living in purity, holiness and honor, man through sin found the ground opening between him and his God, like the separation of the earth in an earthquake. Man could no longer live with his God. Through sin he found himself across a deep chasm or gorge and he had no way in which to return. Man stood helpless with no bridge to cross.

Thus, too, with God. So in His love He made a bridge spanning the vast distance between Himself and helpless man, making it possible for man to return to fellowship with God. That bridge was Christ. Through Christ's incarnate birth, His life of teaching, preaching, example, and finally and most important, through His death and resurrection, Christ became the bridge for man to return to his God. "I am the way, the truth and the life, no man comes unto the Father but by me," says Christ. Man had tried desperately to make this bridge, through self-denial, through fasting, through an attempt to satisfy a Holy God, but holiness demands holiness, and justice demands justice, and man could not measure up. But Christ did, by taking man's burden, paying man's penalty, giving to man His righteousness, offering to live within the heart of man, thus spanning the separation from God.

What a glorious Gospel for a mankind which stands helplessly by seeking a way back to God. What a thrilling story for the sinner who sees his wickedness, finds no power to live as God demands for those in fellowship with Him. Christ is the answer, the bridge, the way back to God.

Few bridges of any kind in all the world are indestructible. One of the world's greatest bridges spans the Golden Gate. Soon after its completion a 75-mile-an-hour hurricane whipped at the bridge and swayed it 12½ feet off its line. It was built to sway 18 feet, and so it stood. But even the greatest of bridges have been destroyed under the power of TNT and aerial bombs——bridges not indestructible.

But this bridge between God and man, who is Christ, is indestructible, open ever for the seeking sinner to find his way back to God. There is no toll house, no requirements of race or color or social standing, only a repentant heart and a seeking faith in this Christ of Calvary. He alone spans the distance between you and your God.

When I was a very small boy, my father, a pastor in Seattle, Washington, took the family on a picnic into the foothills of the Olympic mountains. The car was pulled to a stop just off the roadway and at the edge of a deep gorge. Just beyond lay a beautiful park in the forest. There was just one way to reach it, by a swinging foot-bridge.

I am sure I recall the incident so vividly because of the fear in my little-boy heart as I looked over the cable guard-rail to the rushing river below. It was only the steady hand of my father, and the words, "Don't look down, look across to the park," that gave me the courage to cross.

We, too, as we look at the deep chasm carved by sin, look down and find ourselves afraid. Even the bridge of Christ and His love may leave us fearful. But place your hand in the hand of Christ. Lift your eyes to God's "park" beyond. There you will find the budding leaves of a new life, the fruits of a new faith. You will find the quiet meadows of His peace, the singing birds of His joy, the shelter of His comfort, the sunshine of His eternal goodness.

## SERIOUSLY, NOW...

*For our sake he made him to be sin who knew no sin, so that in him we might become the righteousness of God.* II CORINTHIANS 5:21

There is a captivating story written by an English novelist, Mr. C. E. Montague, to which he has given the title, *Rough Justice*. It tells of little Bron who was brought for the first time to the church where his uncle was vicar. For the boy, this experience was intriguing. The atmosphere quieted him. The organ tones made him sit in wonder. The choir, the prayers, and responses made him strangely alert. Then his uncle stepped into the pulpit and began to preach.

The boy listened intently. It was a strange story that the pastor was telling. It was about a man, the holiest, kindest, and most wonderful who ever lived. Sick people had come to Him and been made well. People terribly sad had been made happy again. People whose lives had been all wrong were forgiven and taught how to forgive others. Folks afraid of dying were promised they could live forever. Because of this man whose name was Jesus, even angry people had become loving.

But not all of them. Some people hated this man Jesus. They wanted to get rid of Him. And they did, or thought they did. They took Him out with two criminals and killed Him on a cruel something called a cross. The uncle went on to say that this man was not dead but lived again; and now He was looking for people who would go out and do for the world what He had done.

The service was over. Worshippers were leaving their pews and moving down the aisles. It was then that the little boy's nurse found that her charge was not by her side. Bron was thoroughly moved by the story of This Man and could not understand why the people around him were so calm about this remarkable happening. They filed out of the church as though nothing strange had been told them. Bron sat in his pew and sobbed. His nurse finally said to him, "Bron, you mustn't take it so much to heart—people might think you are queer."

Perhaps that is just the trouble that you and I have with the story of the cross; that we do not take this remarkable happening to heart; that we too file out of church Sunday after Sunday quite calm over so great an event for us. How often I've wished that I might be hearing that story for the very first time. Perhaps then it could make an impact upon my heart to the degree it did on that little boy's responsive heart. Much too often we with adult minds react more callously to the cross than we do to the heroics of soldier, fireman, or sacrificing parent.

Read again Charles Dickens' *Tale of Two Cities*. You have perhaps forgotten most details in this eighteenth-century story from the French Revolution: the hatred of the commoner for the nobleman; the characters—Vengeance, Jacques Three and Madame De Farge. But it isn't likely that you have forgotten Sydney Carton who, for love of Darnay's Lucy, forcibly changes places with the condemned Darnay in the infamous prison, Conciergerie, in order that Darnay might live. What a story!—one life redeemed by another.

This is the story of our Christ, called by heaven itself the Son of God, One who willingly and innocently went to the cross and death, not out of despairing love as a man might hold for a woman, but out of divine love, exchanging His life for ours. We stand redeemed.

You note that I have used the term "redeemed" rather than "saved" here. I have done so purposely and for emphasis. One can "save" another's life, often without great cost or any particular sacrifice. I may find a man being overcome by gas, and save that man by merely opening the window and calling the rescue squad. The cost to me was really nothing. In another instance, saving the life of someone might involve a tremendous cost, perhaps my own life. That suggests a redeeming—the exchange or giving-up of life to rescue another from death.

Christ *redeemed* you. He suffered, bled, agonized, and then died for you to bring you back from sin, death, and the power of the Devil. In doing so He made it possible for you to "be His own. . . ."

Take a good square look at that story. How can you help being thrilled or sense a tremendous indebtedness! How can you help taking the Cross of Christ *seriously!* "Fear not, for I have redeemed you," says Christ. He might have added, were we to paraphrase His thinking, "Once, in creation, you were destined to belong to God. But you, as all men, came into sin, separating yourself from God. Your natural self is everyday proof of this separation. But God in His love didn't want it that way. You were helpless to do anything about it. Any attempts were like trying to lift yourself off the floor by tugging at your shoelaces. So the Father God stepped in. He sent Me into the world to break the separating barrier of sin, to set you free from enslavement, and to seek to win your heart. I, Christ, did for you what you could not do for yourself. I redeemed you."

"Now there is no longer the insurmountable barrier for you. The Holy Spirit is calling you to claim this redeeming love. He gives the power to claim it. Therefore, with a repentant heart, claim it. If you do, forgiveness and life are yours, for your guilt was carried by Me at the cross, and death was crushed by Me at the open tomb."

Friend, what stark tragedy if, after what Christ in love has done, we deny that redeeming love because "we don't need it." Nothing to me would be more difficult to understand than that God in Christ should die for me, if "I didn't need it." What is often hard for me to understand is *not* that I need Christ's redeeming love, but that He loves me. It was Luther who said, "When I see what kind of a man I am, I do not find it hard to believe in the wrath of God, but I do find it hard to believe in the grace and love of God."

Hard to believe? Yes, but it's true. God says so. "For our sake He made him to be sin who knew no sin, so that in him we might become the righteousness of God." God said so. Christ proves it so.

There are only two places where sin can be: either on your shoulders, and you carry the burden to spiritual death, or on the shoulders of the Savior, and He gives you pardon and *new* life.

# YOU CAN LIVE FOREVER, BEGINNING NOW

*Jesus said to her, "I am the resurrection and the life; he who believes in me, though he die, yet shall he live."*

JOHN 11:25

You can live forever! The fact is that you will. Your soul will, whether you are interested or not. The glory of Easter for the Christian is the *where*.

Physical death for either believer or unbeliever is not a dead-end street, a snuffing out of your spirit's candle. The great difference at death for the unbeliever is the final separation from God. For the believer, it is a final separation from sin to a total life in God. Therefore, the real glory of Easter is that the Christian will live forever with God and without sin; that he can live now with Christ and victor over sin.

This amazing truth stands boldly before you because Jesus Christ on Easter morning "came back again," not a dead Christ but a living Lord. "You killed the Author of life, whom God raised from the dead," preached Peter (Acts 3:15). And *that* changed everything: *Christ raised from the dead.*

European history records an incident when diplomats in attendance at the Congress of Vienna were busily engrossed in remaking the map of Europe. While they were in session, a uniformed courier stepped through the door to announce, "He is back again." "And who is back again?" they inquired. "Napoleon," was the reply. The diplomats had thought themselves quite sanely occupied seeking to anchor Europe's international picture puzzle with Napoleon exiled to Elba. But with this military genius back on the highways of Europe, the international leaders folded their maps and adjourned the conference. Napoleon's marching armies would draw their own new maps.

The enemies of Jesus had been busy redrawing their maps too when the Good Friday sun dropped over the horizon. The followers of Jesus were tearfully occupied with a disappointingly different future, redrawing their maps. Then, with the rising Easter sun, the shout, "He is risen." He is back again. With that, the chart of man's whole future destiny was turned wonderfully upside down. Now man could live forever, beginning now.

"Forever," is an unfathomable word, isn't it? Use a hundred feeble illustrations to describe it in terms of time, and you don't begin to touch the rim of its proportions. But, understandable or not, "forever with the Lord," is the destiny of the followers of Christ. While we know relatively little of "what" is in that future, we do know "Who" is there. That should be enough for any Christian.

Perhaps you wonder at Paul's living with such a sparkling anticipation of "being absent from the body and at home with the Lord." To many this is an exceedingly strange thing. Yet it ought not to be strange for any Christian.

Death held no terror for Paul. He knew that the sting of death was sin and Christ was victor over sin. "Where now, O death, is your power to hurt us? Where now, O grave, is the victory you hoped to win?" (Phillips), are questions simply answered by, "All thanks to God then who gives us the victory through our Lord Jesus Christ."

Even as Christians, too many of us fail to catch the real meaning of this. How apt we are to borrow from the world its thinking about death and treat the death of other Christians as something tragic. But this was not the attitude of the early church. They marched singing to the cemetery, carrying a loved one who "faithful unto death" had claimed "the crown of life."

Christ, you see, had taken real death out of dying. The soul lived on now with God, totally free from sin, and the body in eternity's timelessness would soon be raised a glorified body. Eternity for the Christian spirit had already begun in Christ in this life.

Early in the Christian era, a number of believers had been enslaved and forced to serve in the mines of North Africa. Living almost like moles in the earth and given but few hours above ground in the sun and rain, one would have expected their spirits to have become quite numb, their hopes dimmed out. But inscribed on the walls of the underground tunnels were the words, *"Vita! Vita! Vita!"—"Life! Life! Life!"* Even in a "living death," they knew *life.*

For the Christian, eternity begins *now.* It began in fact at that awesome moment when Jesus Christ claimed your heart. Beginning then, it will never end. Physical death, as we know it, will not stop it. Nothing will.

It is this which changes a mere existence to real living in this world. Are you bored with life? If you are, something is wrong. I sat one noon hour chatting with a most successful business man. He was exceedingly wealthy, had a large mansion, several cars, a family, and a good reputation. One of his comments as we visited was that he was "bored to death"; yes, bored in spite of money, family, travel, security, success and all the rest. Here was a man who, as silly as it would sound to many, was just existing. He hadn't discovered life.

Jesus ran into the same thing. Recall the man who requests of Jesus that He speak to his brother that he might divide the inheritance with him. Jesus' reply was in the form of a rebuke, "My dear man," He said, "who appointed me a judge or arbitrator in your affairs? . . . A man's real life has nothing to do with how much he possesses" (Phillips).

No, real life isn't to be found there, no matter how high you pile "things." But it can be found, and is found, in a personal relationship to God through Christ. This relationship produces real life and, as a result, real living, now.

Here then is life "hid with God in Christ," eternal life. Here is real living with a sense of meaningfulness and direction. Losing the self-life, you find the Christ-life. Immortality is stamped on your soul, and all of life now becomes related with a new perspective to all of remaining eternity.   81